T0208231

MAGNIFICENT
CHAOS

MATTHEW PUTMAN

ILLUSTRATIONS BY MARINE PUTMAN

authorHOUSE®

AuthorHouse™
1663 Liberty Drive
Bloomington, IN 47403
www.authorhouse.com
Phone: 1-800-839-8640

First published by AuthorHouse 2/21/2011

ISBN: 978-1-4567-4352-9 (e)
ISBN: 978-1-4567-4351-2 (sc)

Library of Congress Control Number: 2011902560

Printed in the United States of America

Any people depicted in stock imagery provided by Thinkstock are models, and such images are being used for illustrative purposes only. Certain stock imagery © Thinkstock.

This book is printed on acid-free paper.

The 20th century physicist Erwin Schrödinger was the poet of modern science. Working in metaphor, he bridged his profound knowledge of physics, and his interest in biology with poetry. After reading all of his descriptions of the atom, and the cell, we are left with an overwhelming sense of the fragile cohesion that holds us together. The universe expands towards entropy, or chaos. This is inevitable. So how do we explain animal evolution, which is prone to simplification, through Natural Selection? This is where Schrödinger made a philosophical leap, which most scientists accept as a likely answer. He proposed that if there is increased order in a system, then there will be increased entropy outside of it. This explains why most cells are not cancerous. The chaos surrounds, rather than encompasses it.

By considering the universe in ourselves, it is not such a far reach to intuit the big bang, the most dramatic explosion of chaos, which ultimately placed us here. The early universe and its future are the domains of astrophysicists, cosmologists and biologists. Our bodies are the labs of the same. Consciousness is still a mystery. It is a sense rather than a science. If then our consciousness is chaos, our poems are the cellular order that balances it.

These particular poems were mostly written during a time in my life when balancing order and chaos was most important. In 2006 I was going through chemotherapy for esophageal cancer, finishing a Ph.D. in Applied Physics and, most importantly, getting to know my newborn baby girl Juliette. These three experiences were impossible to rationalize simultaneously. No matter the powerful parallel processes of the brain, birth, career and impending death, just seem too distant to mingle with over cocktails. These poems provide abstract bridges. They are an emerging scientist's flow through entropic despair and worry towards coherence in an ever expansive universe of the mind.

CHAPTER 1
ENTANGLEMENT

Counterpoint

Ok to tell the truth I didn't want to write in A minor
As Alicia knows with no black keys
I can close my eyes.

A temporary adjustment to the system
Failed for long cycles
Of Mendelssohn and molestations

In a tinder box of nitrogen, and water.

Tomorrow I will row from the Seine to Staten Island
Where on minimal blue dusk nights
I can doze off without the sound

Of pumping factories of minerals like mollusks.

As I approach the keyboard, I invert the sound
Reaching over entrails of ivory
Towards the dark major

Where an E flattens to infinity.

Frontier

On a distant planet where the Rockies crumble onto the plains
They talk of Orion and grizzlies taken by dead presidents
And pardonable lies, which are scooped up in the big dipper
Where a virgin cries in English, holding a daydream of things to come.

Pinnacle

Onboard those of us salute
of what is locked unconsciously beneath.
A tiny morsel reflects quanta in the day or night.

Undermined is the lapsed view
of a mid age 30ish man.
A fantasy too small to see,
    Too large to Comprehend.

A dead genius limping past my window.
Miles above the ground a planet I don't recognize.

Pittering drops wiped away.
Pattering footsteps I can't identify.

If night comes again
I won't reach up or bend down,
But grasp the nearest star
And run with her into my field.

Renewal

I hear the starlings singing in German
and don't remember a word you
said to me last night in my dream.
A new dialect.
Some grin I recognize
having never seen.

I hear a chirp again in Russian,
How far you have traveled at
An altitude just above the
Japanese maple
Or Seagram Tower.

Some mulled cocktail of
Gatorade, honey and tears.
Sweeter than ever that voice.

I want to sing and cry beside you
at the fallen wood,
beside the lodge.

Shape From Shading

A pattern can propagate in all continents, and at sea.
Checked in for too many days doodling in board rooms and BMWs
While another pianist zips through standards with the left hand while sipping
Something that changes color in the sun.
These waves and dots disappear only at the edges where
Infinities begin to tear apart bodies in the black hole of being.

All Paris lights up with sustainability, in a now frostless climate
North of Maine.

Too opposed to putting my hat on the table I hold it in my lap.
Flipping it invisibly up and down and wishing it were weighted for such occasions.
I see the distance, where the pattern dissipates, there is only a child dancing like Cunningham
To a vacant sound, which pushes her on a lyrical sail boat journey.

How can I who cannot swim pull her back from the sea of paradise at the rim of knowledge
To a table where food is served in courses and eaten with ancient utensils.
The rhythms of the tides. The sounds in a vacuum and a last perfect leap will crash down,
As we grasp tightly the corners of our chairs, and get lost in the repetition.

Song of the Urban Thrush

Sounding a tad tormented for nothing.
I think.
Nowhere is a café it, but on a street with a French name.
Unfortunately trapped in Brooklyn, where wifi works better than the espresso machines.
Timeless is the desire to remain anonymous and seen.
Spiritually centered, but in control.
Maximum roller riding coaster crazed, on smoothly re-asphalted side streets.
Punctuality for monotony keeps the stay short.
Walking past countless fronts of old brick structures where
martinis and Sam Adams are sold.
Wanting a tumbler of house red, finding only a short stem growing tasteless conformity.
Musically speaking, thirty years is too short and too long.
Mind floats above boroughs to Burroughs where a racing mind can rest with sounds;

    birds,
    blues,
    A binge of imagination.

Synaptic Melody

Microscopic divisions bringing unity
In mornings of strange serenity.
Bitterness sweet, same of the cold
As a warmness flows.
A reassuring spa through veins, our soul?
Unsure.

Cerebral efficiency with little electrical loss.
Closer to sacrifice.
100 or so degrees shouts still not registering
Through cacophonous populous buzz.

Maybe a few chords,
Notes,
A Whisper at 3 AM,
An arm around the waste
Resonate.

Transforms

Sinusoidal silence of conditioning
Impossible to hear or see,
I feel.

An unconscious ticking of desires,
Cell divisions,
Entangling.

Tunneling or hopping I reach
A train, a field,
A mirrored skyscraper.

A knock or a twitch
Reminds me of the never resting
State of being.

Yo-Yo

Wound tightly around the steering wheel,
I lean over and touch her hand.
Wound around my fingers
Loops I cannot find either beginning or end.
Wound up inside a cashmere scarf,
I cannot see her pensive fear.
Wound up in electric coils,
I gently warm as my blood boils.
Wound up gray matter
Doesn't divide, move or clatter.
Wound up strings and skin
Inside homes of carpet and tin.

CHAPTER 2
FROM THE BOTTOM UP

After Life

Directly into a pin prick of a hole a liquid.
Not as fast as light or even sound, I wonder when it will arrive.
To heat the heart and cool the misfiring of neural panic.
Still I don't find a light too common.

Colors are all that I want.
Going into the blues in the night become black, and burned out retinas relax.
Tragic films at first loved, are feared upon second viewing.
A scene once provided a chuckle, now brings a chill.

A dropper like a hammer
Breaking down matter into molecules,
Molecules into atoms,
Atoms into an abyss.

Brooklynite

Before it crashed
this party gathered dust
on stoves and mantles
pre-google books
stacked feet high
towards the elevated
crackling of the second floor parlor.
Pushing funny faced
Dance divas,
Poker player,
Wall Street , Main Street Mavens
Sat unconcerned that the reds of
the Chagall were fading to pink
even in a grayed version
of that once white room.
Where carpenters
Drank unknown lager,
And posing in Levi's fashion
Painters with mice
replace painters with oil
and drink Brooklyn beer of five dollars.

Decorum

The dirt is underneath the Pansy print
In the Hilton hallway.
A must for a night mulling ideas.
With groans from fucking,
Scents of bourbon.

My thoughts equidistant from the moon.
A radius of an angstrom
Or light year.
Always on the tip of the tongue.

The bud droops.
Tastes dull.
A punch annihilates the
Somber panic
Of another night

Under a duvet in summer.

Jump Drive

Time to Flash memory
    Into mega pixels.
Time to Capitulate
    Copulate
    Corrupt
    Change Letters.
Time to render obsolete
    Photos of bearded men
    Quilts of dead widows
    Houses with fake shutters.
Time to sleep in for once.
    More water
    More crackers
    A comfortable pair of slippers.
Time to break the fucking clock.
    The flickering lamp.
    The old vase.

Memorial Day

Crossing himself by the chapel
he sipped an ale and panted
as he passed days
after Dartmouth lacrosse
matches long ended
and the last volunteer soldier fell
from pneumonia that comes in the 80's.
When last picked, once piled apples,
rot by wagons
of yellow, advertised taxis
with swipe cards and
piss stains reminder of
the park for 20 summers.
Heat hampers the block
but he shivers as the
light from Farrels
goes out.
Cars make way for street cleaning.

Newscast

A boxing car in my way on the road on May evenings.
Clashing sickles into a normal mood
Fresh, fantasy, frequency frantic.
Pulling harder, making no progress.
Reaching into a pit to find only dark air.
Some strange crack in this rock seems to penetrate.
Not recoil.
Not revisit.
A war it seems is only as far as the light coming through the wall.
Bombs though are cold, and quiet when muted to hear
Cars honking, dogs barking and my baby crying.
Too often mumbling to myself a personal victory is only one drop,
One pill, or one kiss away.
Waiting for the fire to start up seems like hours in the moments,
Thousands of ks per beat.
Syncopated and flickering the chaos is kept at arms length.
Away from the wall.
The head,
The heart.

Night Fryer

Pressing round noir midnight at midday
Hops of bubbling froth hop from
Point of longing to tastes lingering,
Imports without much conditioning from vents,
Air or otherwise.

What unreasonable directions from pulpits
Tarnished white crackled
On sets above bars of malts.
Sinking into uncomfortable relaxation.
Ponder dreary dreams, destroyed only.

Snippets of grease strained trust
On pages not fitting to print
To pour the warm finish
Over the tender crisp skin
Remains glued.

Old Man Ebbits

It whistled like the pine needle and cone,
In mid spring, on some back corner, of my amygdale.
When I saw through my closed eyes an old
Church, which someone seemed new, with
The houses and children stinking and crackling
By the walks of neat life episodes.
In pale blues, not yet able to fade to grey
And knowing that a colorful rainbow of
Prosperity was yesterday's ball game
And today's racing form, lies marked and
Crumbled on the bathroom floor of Farrells.
The drugstore glasses scratched.
The watch face ruined, like nails and
Tails where serpents exist alongside rats
On subways where the road to a park was
Long since bulldozed.

Speed Bump

Into a hole on Seventh, I penetrate too deep.
Illusions of a bottom that I can't make out.
Geometric in format.
Algebraic in symmetry with the far horizon of the sea somewhere.
An Allegory. A hypothesis, a lost sentence.
Musical in skies, but buried underneath the sticky stale asphalt.
Human animal kind, not nice.
Starvation in classes, of class not distinguishing.
Too many yellow lines painted to close to see from here.
Too many mysteries too far to solve.
I look again inside the hole and realize that it must never be filled.

The Excuse

Blame it on the pen,
The paper
The room
The car.

Blame it on the dark cloud
Bright again
Too loud.

Blame girls no girl.
A blank page
Too full to tear
Too empty to fill.

Blame my ear sight
Nose bleed
Nerve endings in my toes.

Blame the keys
The reeds
The picks
The hole.

Blame a cursed fish stew
Blackened battered
Crumbling cold.

Blame the States Scotch
The Belgian beer
The French vodka
The valium
The joint.

Blame the absence of Absinthe.

Vanilla Coffee

A Portrait Of Ronnie

Sidewalk sense, from prospect to fifth
He always walks with a Brooklyn cowboy stride.
Speaking of horses, he has rode from the Crown Heights corner to
To Grand Army plaza, and back to Pritchett square.
Where yuppies roller blade, and homeless men grunt good morning.
Where girls dark and light wave hello, and smile.
"The one over there polished my knob in 78, in the parking lot
Of a disco on 87th."
He drinks a vanilla coffee for 2 hours each morning.
He collects plastic, sanitized utensils.
He has pockets full of napkins.
He solves the Daily News puzzle like rain man calculates birthdays.
He wipes my little girl's face, and sings her Britney.
He plans to fish from the peer, and float all day on a boat.
He heads to the Off Track betting.
Gripping a funny cigarette between giant callused fingers.
Without speaking an r, his tongue slides through
A hole left empty where two stained teeth used to be.
He stops by an old, new brownstone
Greets the Jewish millionaire, and offers his services.
Painting, roofing, or any fucking thing you need.
A dollar, or two hundred will get him back to breakfast.
Out of the one room closet where
He tunes his antenna to watch alligators and the Mets.
Ten calls a day to Dulce, and Laura,
Family stuck an ocean of broken down subways, and potholed streets away
in Williamsburg.
Looking toward the Brooklyn Bridge, a better day is coming.
To share a two bedroom home, and bring in Barbeque.
To wake up together, and both of our families sip
Vanilla Coffee for two hours.

Walk-Up

The dense wood beams
Firmly sway and slowly burn
Keeping lives in tiny third floor flats
Where windows work better than pipes.
Cable brings the world of 2009.
Beside certain particular, particulier
Where status stood, in luxury
Where the shit from the street
Is hidden by clay,
Oil
And rose vases of mint.
The song of pigeons and stews stirs
The sort of pensive hours
Of waiting for sunlight to pass
Into a perfusion of sonic whispers.
Stones still harboring perversions of eternity
While all slowly erode
Into pieces of next year.

CHAPTER 3
ILLUMINATION

Blue

When the rumble stops
    Cells cool.

When motion accelerates
    Flora bleed.

When time is short
    Humans panic.

When clothes don't protect,
    Air strikes comfort.

When chromatics startle
    Arpeggios console

When colorless tones confuse
    Blue diverts.

Happy Hour

Is there chatter of the stupid man
who vomits three times?
One the remaining wine.
Two the squats and curls.
Three the day long shaking of
life less meaningful than expected.

Holiday

Unattached and Swaying,
I took a shot and
Waited for the
Storm after the calm.

Where a flip of a pancake
Or a comment
Lands somewhere between
The lips and the bowels.

Where plastic chairs
Melt rather than fade
Rather than tarnish
Under a shrinking star

In an expanding universe.

Where a child can only taste
An acid drop.
Not the clear snow
On a mountain of springs
And winters

Of scalding indifference.

Luxury

Designer vodka by the gallon.
Gigabyte Strayhorn melodies
Shuffled and woven
Through southern suffering
And old world comfort.

Stark chaise
Memory foam
Holding solitary untouching forms
In King Size fashion.

Rips in an aura and sewn together.
Pretension and power pills.

Taxis scented with mideastern spice.
Guarded by plastic,
Rear seat chatter and IPOD drone.

A patch of hair fallen
From poison and inertia.
Covered by cashmere and
The dream of growth.

Monochrome

I missed the chance to shower
and now feel a creep up my back
when clowns pass me.
I regret the moments of endless
Smiling,
Laughing.

Wanting more to dwell in a deep bunker.
Bombs dropping, but not bursting my gaze.
Downward onto a yellowed dust covered page.
Where words blend more than pop.
Expressions are muted.
Sounds unseen.

Still not blind, hypersensitive
To shades of contempt from those above.
Buried neighbors.
Shy cousins climbing trees
To look down at the
Mutation of our souls.

Night Light

A Cramp in the right foot toes,
A truck passes.
An Owl moans.
A Cricket chirps

My Baby Laughs.

A Trip Trek ticking
A mile per second
As bio rhythms pattern
Victorious song.

The sun gets edges that
The mountain loses.
Moon mysteries for
Her Young processes
Of a heart not slowed by cynicism.

On the First Day of Christmas

Of the shopping Christmas dad
Skeptics learn multitudes from pigeon songs
Cooing over the Trash bin, and forcing our eyes,
Towards ellipses of gold and red, which
Firing through the optical nerve and landing in the void
Where the esophagus and heart flutter together
In a cushion of snowflakes that life is real.
So with a scarf, cashmere, the orchestral triangular
Bellowing the ping under the coat, and hiding the pulse
Of a detracted science teacher, remembering his Grandmas
Experiment of love.
Resting alone on the stool, the chatter turned to clamor up
A bill that list a debt too large to compile, as summations fail
To infinity, instead existing in a theoretical haze.
To rise now, with high pulse, low anxiety, and arms raised
To the North Pole.

Pre-dusk

Too often lacking of rhythm in a warm room,
Neither becomes bleak blathering, unlikely, fresh fume.
When looking past the false formalities,
Blown out new century gas lights reminiscent fake qualities.
A tool is not so much a hammer as a chip,
Inserted behind the letters, frig, ear or clip.

With aided glance of burb lights under roofs of foam,
Hoping that Brooklyn is still Whitman's home.
Not wanting it to be his house on the east banks,
Carved, too high ceilings , brimming emotionless flanks.
Parks are full of cars, and cars full faint smells and matches flickering
Not lost in memory but in having never been teetering, trembling.

To modularize modernity is only to be human.
Predate a word not a soul or stance in other world's lumen.
The light will not burn forever no matter the many times lit.
The building will crumble, happily spent.
The mortgage not withstanding a typhoon of investment rot.
The sky still hangs over for some new thought.

Propulsion

Boeing 717 slipping into a Rothco
Primary colors split in the sky.
Popping incandescence below,
Not Yet Starry at 7.
Serene and solitaire.

What mirrors or miles.
Streaming sunsets underneath.
A sign or song.
Sung of sinusoidal flickering flux.

Reaching me from a future
Not destroyed or reconstructed.
Only light beaming in,
A frequency of sublime propulsion.

Red

Wishing to imagine a red.
I write in rhythm uncommon.
The lost art of science of soul.
The rouge of roe or hoe
Or any other thought which
Holiday and hatred derive.

A carpet exists for me.
Coating a room.
Black and white.
Technicolor Cinemascope of
Paradise.

Dressing as a child in a pajama
I rose in rows of red to be a devil.
Never knowing how prophetic the fantasy.

Sense of Smell

She wants a wider rim
on the glass filled with Margaux
as she finds the scent more
sensual than the taste.
Like lavender in fields
Or roses in bottles.
Orgasms reached in the nostrils
Of naïve children of 30.
Wanting more than midnight
Conversation or games of cards.
When minstrels sing
And miseries turn away
The sun of glowing diamond watches.
Time flies and burgundy flows
Under the bridge to an oblique
Powder and spice.

Night Chill

I slept with ear buds last night
To alter dreams, or push them
In directions more appealing
than the terror of normal sleep
of goblins from a future of emptiness.
Replacing fears of now only for moments before
I crash to wakefulness.
Instead Satie variations repeat
To complete a rest, normally of
Itching torment, now peaceful
Pulses of the first of floating
Bass notes in an octave
Elevated above the heart.
Chimes of Steinway song, remind
Me of a cool compress which
Stopped the swelling of my strain.
A misstep, in perfect harmony,
Of my pillow, my love, my calm,
On notes that smother out conviction
Of prudence.

CHAPTER 4
NATURAL SELECTION

Anchor

Excuses from Sapphire
Only hearing Sirens and beeps.
Little Language or laughter in between
the coughs, a mind roaring to wake.

A heart burning to sleep.
Peace making, troubleshooting star.
Searching for an orchard of apples
Fallen, nibbled by sparrows rising.

Turned over twice.
A spine twisted to touch a stone,
Smoother than
Toe nails, beer bottles, a finger in the eye.

Prominence not deserved.
Providence on an island,
Exposed on one side to waves.
Crashing and filling mucus with salt.

The body half empty and half full.
The rock held together,
By ionic fusion
A moonless night.

At The Trough

Everyday a new apparition
descends an escalator
with Gucci white loafers,
and denim denoting a free mode.
Like jazz standards and soldiers
parading past lines of
fast food Chinese and Mexican.
Minding our way as
Orders become orders.
Brown remains brown.
Black remains Black.
Pop solitary sessions
in ears that are
no more twirls and turns
towards the brain.
But teleportations to the mind.

Blues For Alberto

Racing thinking and too much blinking.
Feeling dripping more mind than spine.
An enduring delight in lifting,
In swinging further and faster,
With an occasion to sneak
Protected body upper cutting.

Spontaneous like the notes of an improv.
Planned like a concerto.

Never twitching while moving;
Electrons jutting around active centered atoms.
Paralyzed but dizzy. A Flu.
Strong and powerful, poignant movements
In flight with no fear.
Lazy in mind, making stronger bodies.

Neurons breaking and building in simultaneous three minutes.
Looking for inside spirit on a:
Treadmill,
A Ring
A Hospital Bed

A punching drunk now wide awake
Observer of slow time in fast motion.
A life at 32 not dwindling for
The first rounds of this eternal bout.
Combustible, Caving, Crushing and Cursing.
Left to old time pondered simple patience.

Like the Dali Lama in a mediation.
A squirrel scrambling and hopping from branches.
No time for nightmares,
In the moment of burning life and certain TKOS.

Hibernation

Padlocked inside a duffle
With a wisp of oxygen I squirm.

Inside a tomb of drywall south exposure
With a window box I strip.

Corpuscles of sweat, underneath a flannel
With coolness in eternal I cough.

Glass ovals, mirrored bathrooms,
My mind ending before my feet

I glimpse a region of snow covered pines
Where crashed planes and starving fish

Go to die.

Hunt and Gather

Farming in Brooklyn on an Autumn morning.
Leaning across traffic to notice a wrinkle of herb.
Fresh strands and strains my eyes.
Beauty coalescing in drops around the sewer.

Savoring miles of torment in microns of tension.
I looked at a needle lying next to the hair barrette.
Seeing the pick ax of a long life of 30 something years.
Piling on papers with bold text of nonsense.
Agri-light, municipal stagnation.

A border between the work and the wealth.
A comma, between the then and new.
A coffee to invigorate and relax
A bullet for a point, or a chance.
A missile to defend and detect.
A child to scream and silence our fears.

Marsh

Mixed morphologies of herb
Blend in a distant memory
Without horizon.
When did we touch
The crust around
the fractals of a sea,
where fish float fins up?
Muscles rot in the peek of
Daylight and
Rise with waves at night.

Migrant

While a stale scent wakes me
On a train car crowded and clean.
Only a rustle of three countries of papers
Predict gloom
Turned over cars and stomachs.

The globe twirls
And a man crosses his legs.
Only breath touches, torches
A path towards the East.

Past the layer highways of
Generations milling, sewing
And stamping.

Now pondering on a superhighway
Only three seconds from daylight at midnight.

Mille Pas

Two long centimeters of soil
And a small frog appears,
Looks at my girl and I,
And retreats into the hole
Under the rock.

Shards of Old cans
Up Root our yet to be flowers.
A day of rain is not long enough
To topple the last moss stone
Past our little home.

Where dust settles
In the Autumn
Winds pass,
Like centuries for a star.

Penniless

For years I wore pennies in my loafers.
A laugh from some.
Respect of old school ideals from others.
Scorn from the displaced former middle with no class.
A judgment too harsh and unsatisfying.

Really no one cares until a penny falls out.
One remaining.
The question of timing and rebirth presents a quandary of sorts.
I removed the remaining cent and walked up Broadway
looking for a shine.

Sharp Knives

Cutting Melons
On a terrace.

Cutting, Carving red,
White and grays.

Cutting Time out
Of a map.

Cutting classes of
Race and elements.

Cutting cloth
From naked street addicts.

Cutting Hair
From Chemo patients and bald blonds

Cutting a ripe onion
Until we weep by the board.

Small Print

Possible Side Effects Include;
Simultaneous combustion of internal organs and outside perceptions.
Miserable convulsing trembling peace in hours passing.
Shiny Streets after Raindrops fall instead of gloomy grey roads.
Nausea and Vomiting
Euphoria
Early Dementia.

Needles may cause pain,
    may dull life
    may release endorphins,
        hormones
        adrenaline bursts.

I will not swallow.
I will not breath.
I will not shoot an arrow.
Only lie down next to a dream
    And Cry.

Terminal

To let in Oxygen
I need to take a breath.
A plane in flight doesn't ventilate.

A nerve shock through
Axons of pulsating flashes.
The first kindling in a fire
Now burning in a constant stream
Of current to my heart.

I wince and glance
To wonder where I have gone
Since taking off my hat and
Leaving a part of me behind the Ticket Counter.

Vagabondage

Seasick inside the air-conditioned closed tight chamber.
A dusk has already settled.
Time's miniscule reductionist ways.

Marked as Always by a Flab,
    An Unkempt Whisker,
An Arm streaked red on the temple.

All is gained in tremulous waters,
    Sunny days expose a grit uncommon,
In northern climates, less elevated above the heart.

Innocence is the only thing left, right,
The romance of novels at night.
Mischievous consciously cool and connives.

I want to touch the mattress
The Pillow
The Sky
You.